Concrete Paradise

poems by

Brian Dunlap

Finishing Line Press
Georgetown, Kentucky

Concrete Paradise

Copyright © 2018 by Brian Dunlap
ISBN 978-1-63534-626-8 First Edition
All rights reserved under International and Pan-American Copyright Conventions. No part of this book may be reproduced in any manner whatsoever without written permission from the publisher, except in the case of brief quotations embodied in critical articles and reviews.

ACKNOWLEDGMENTS

"A Simple Game" – published in *CCM-ENTROPY*
"Not Enough" – *Muse*
"Human" – *Angel City Review*
"At Ocean Park Beach" – *California Quarterly*
"Shared Language" – *Statement Magazine*
"A Roof Over Their Heads" – *Writers Resist*
"Who Call This Home" – The Table Reading Series zine *Create Nurture Sustain*
"Those Who Came Before Us" – *december*, winner of 2018 Jeff Marks Memorial Poetry Prize

Publisher: Leah Maines
Editor: Christen Kincaid
Cover Art: Brian Dunlap
Author Photo: Scott Dunlap
Cover Design: Elizabeth Maines McCleavy

Printed in the USA on acid-free paper.
Order online: www.finishinglinepress.com
also available on amazon.com

Author inquiries and mail orders:
Finishing Line Press
P. O. Box 1626
Georgetown, Kentucky 40324
U. S. A.

Table of Contents

A Land Etched in Past Lives 1

L.A. River 3

Human 4

A Simple Game 5

Shaped by Its Streets 8

Not Enough 10

Oakwood 12

Those Who Came before Us 15

Human Geography 17

At Ocean Park Beach 19

An Hour and a Half 'Till Sunrise 20

Who Call This Home 22

A Roof over Their Heads 27

Shared Language 29

*For my parents Scott and Terri Dunlap,
thanks for everything*

A Land Etched In Past Lives

       I

I am a second generation Angeleño,
who has passed my mother's high school
so often I've lost count. Uni High
carrying little known Tongva
history. My mother's history
left in Michigan. A place
I've never been.

      II

In Michigan,
my mother visited the family
farm, where her own mother,
as a young girl, gathered eggs
in the early dawn. Where my mother
grew close to her sweet Aunt Dorothy,
a woman still wed
to that land, a land
my mother left.

      III

I drive through a land etched
in past lives, where I
have carved my personal history.
I pass Kuruvunga Springs,
Uni High, where
natural fresh water gave
birth to a Tongva village.
Where Father Serra
led mass with the natives
six years before the thirteen colonies
declared their independence. Where I arrived
at the crack of dawn on a Saturday,
as a senior,
tired and cold,
to take the SAT.

IV

In my hands is my great
grandmother's stained and worn
first year reader. Carefully turning the fragile
and loose pages I'm turning back time.
I find written before the title page
some of her last surviving handwriting:
Miss Ester Marten 5.
Handwriting over a hundred
years old. Find the land stamped
on a tiny sticker on the inside
back cover:
Dunning's Vicksburg, Mich.

The L.A. River

Los Ángeles is no longer remembered
as a city built
along a river's
life giving water.
Man defiled nature,
the river's banks molded into concrete.

Across the river's banks,
interlocking L.A. spray painted
in big, white box letters.
Names outlined in red,
spray painted over light blue.

Young men from a broken country
where "all men are created equal"
rings hollow through their
forgotten sections of Los Ángeles-Watts,
El Sereno, Vermont Knolls.
Where the promises of government
for equal schools
involves being buzzed in through a metal gate
claiming it's for their safety
before they're afforded their right
to the halls of knowledge.

The trickle of L.A. River
continues to survive hot,
dry summers. Tags
along its banks, a connection.
Together they say:
"Look.
       See us.
              We're still here."

Human

In Guatemala
gangs and police take young girls,
rape them,
throw them in plastic bags.
It's not safe for them anymore.

Law enforcement, the judicial system,
all run by men.
Sexual violence historically downplayed,
normalized, disinclined to preserve justice,
afraid to implicate themselves.

A homeland with failing institutions,
with a homegrown revolution
in the shadows of the Second World War.
1940s. Democratization.
For land reform.
To rein in the oligarchy, U.S. corporations
that made them a banana republic.
Crushed with help from the CIA.
No democracy here. It ran in opposition
to U.S. interests in someone else's
homeland.

For 30 years,
from the ashes of American intervention,
the Guatemalan army rampaged
through its borders, raping,
murdering,
in the name of Communism.
Reached the western highlands. Ran a
war of genocide against the indigenous Maya.
It wasn't safe for them anymore.

Now, young girls flee.
Sin nombre.
Through brush.
Through city streets.
Hopping trains in Mexico.
Sin nombre.
Across the hot scorching Sonora,
through the brown waters of the Rio Grande.

From a broken country.
Wanting only to be considered human.

A Simple Game

> I

At a year and a half,
Fatima's eyes are wide and wondrous.
Her cheeks are rosy on her pale skin.
And Mar Vista Park seeps into her touch,
the assessment of her movements,
the excitement
as she waddles after her tennis ball.

Watching Fatima,
her mother wears a hajib
that hides her hair, a long
dress that covers her legs.
But all I see
is a toddler
with the world laid out before her.

Possibilities
to explore.
                    Possibilities yet
                    unknown.

> II

We—America—have chosen
to run from our history,
never reconcile with our nation's past.
We have never learned
of The Exclusion Act of 1882,
Chinese in America ineligible
for citizenship. No other country
except Nazi Germany and South Africa
withheld naturalization
on purely racial grounds.

We've forgotten Japanese internment
since every Japanese in America

was a spy,
an enemy alien,
collaborating with Japan
to overthrow the United States
and spread Fascism in America.

      III
The tennis ball sits in the sandbox.
The little girl stares at the ball,
stares at the sand. Fatima squats,
hesitates. Then reaches out,
her tiny arm too short.

She looks back at her mother,
brief concern in her eyes.
But I step in, sweat band around
my forehead, running shoes on my
feet.

Gently, I hand Fatima her ball,
cheeks still rosy on her pale skin,
and say in a sweet voice,
      "Here you go."

With a timid expression on her face,
Fatima quickly toddles
towards her mother, throws the ball
and gives chase.

Wonder,
at such a simple game.

Shaped By Its Streets

Born and raised
in Los Ángeles,
I've been shaped
by its streets.
Its patchwork quilt
of multiple cultures
fusing inside me.

As a high school senior, the original
white of my ancestors mixed
with the Chicano world
of my first love. Of an abuelita
who could speak no
English. Of words I needed
translated. The Spanish slang
my ex used for certain items—
chonies, chanklas—a normal part
of her vocabulary.

Music that pours from my car stereo
is a tapestry of its neighborhoods.
The Latin of the Eastside—son
jarocho blending with rock and Cuban
Charanga with Spanglish
lyrics on top of cumbia—of Quetzal,
of La Santa Cecelia, of Las Cafeteras.
The white middle class angst
of punk rock played by
Valley band Bad Religion with the funk
infused rock of Red Hot Chili Peppers.
Or the deep, laid back beats
of gangster rap rising
from the streets of South Central,
from Compton,
angry at the system. Notes and lyrics
vital and alive. A normal
part of my everyday world.

But it's the friends I've made,
who have a mother from Taiwan or a father
from England, who are half
German and Salvadoran, who moved
to Los Ángeles from
a suburb of Detroit, moved to L.A.
as a teenager
from the Philippines,
who are native Angeleños and transplants,
where I grew up
understanding the world
as lives I recognized, L.A.s
that are familiar, but not
mine.

      So, I have never felt comfortable
in a completely white world. More
comfortable learning a Taiwanese
ritual where the deceased's bedroom
remains untouched for a year
after death, preserving their
essence, allowing the spirit
to go to the next life peacefully.
Of attending open mics
in Latino neighborhoods, knowing
the words will be more necessary,
confronting the most difficult subjects,
that truly speak
to who we are.

Born and raised in Los Ángeles,
I've been shaped by its streets.
Its patchwork quilt
        gifting me a night with friends
embarrassing ourselves
            at Kelly's house
                to the k-pop version
                    of *Just Dance*.

Not Enough

I see too many lives
discarded. People forgotten.
Where have the angels gone?
    Where are the Angeleños who care
about the lives on skid row?

The anonymous stoic faces,
the empty, downcast eyes.
Those treated as invisibles
    shuffling from rescue mission
to rescue mission, with hopes for a
meal or an empty cot. Just a roof
over their heads at night.
Turned away for another evening.

There are not enough facilities
in this paradise.

In a city where a billionaire
has built his own art museum,
a space to display the art he
owns, in a city that for decades
delayed the Purple Line subway
that would bring desperate relief
to Wilshire, the country's most congested
boulevard—too many NIMBYs—Tuberculosis
has spread through skid row, lives
confined by court rulings
to a slowly shrinking number
of downtown streets.

Where have the angels gone?
    What happened to the wisdom
we were taught as young children,
that wrapped around how we
first knew how to treat
others?

The mental hospitals have long
been shut. Patients with schizophrenia,
paranoia, left to the streets, supports
of family insignificant, severed.

I pass homeless encampments under the 405,
see Latinos pushing shopping carts
with recyclable cans and bottles.
In Culver City's vibrant
arts district, black men are
curled up in nooks
and crannies of storefronts,
as a lone white man, his clothes
the color of the gray grime
of the streets, twice each day,
works out at Mar Vista Park.

Yet, on the city's eastside,
in the Aliso-Pico Gardens projects,
Father Greg Boyle connects with vatos.
He listens to their stories,
their worries, and from decades
sharing the same streets,
these young Latinxs
listen to his words. He fills the gaps,
preventing another troubled teen
from living on the streets.

Oakwood
> *black since the time of Abbot Kinney. 1905.*

Oakwood Rec Center:
Thin film of dried sweat
covers my skin.
Summer 2014.

Deep thump of base emanates
from the picnic tables, from the reunion,
thuds off and between
homes that encircle the park.

Loud full laughter from a shared
memory between cousins.
A plastic beer cup
gripped in one hand,
the storyteller, his hand—warm, knowing—
rests on his cousin's shoulder.

"Hey girl! How you doin?"
rises from the rap,
a woman in a tangerine jumpsuit
embracing with the tight warmth of a relative.
Their deep shared history,
wide smiles across lips,
brightness in their eyes, saying all
that words can't.

When I turn the corner
a cop car, the LAPD,
eye of gentrification,
stopped at the fringes. At the corner,
feet from the reunion.
*****

Residents in Oakwood used to know
each neighbor.
Family.
Community.

Older people sat on front porches,
experience in their gaze,
over 7th,
over Indiana,
a hard tenderness in their
watchful eyes, a village
to raise their children.

Today, homes
in the midst of being remolded
sit behind green canvas-covered
chain-link, shadows
across the hollow frames.
Remodeled homes:
hard, 90 degree angles—in shades of gray—
jut out in cold rectangles or squares.
Fences enwrap lives
in cocoons of isolation,
the street at arms' length.

While under the high California sky,
parked on the other side of the benches,
a small tight group of black men
crowd around a classic
purple, Impala convertible. A low-rider,
its lines crisp, body clean,
ready for a night of cruising,
that is no longer allowed.
It rises up, down, at
slight, jerky angles
still retaining its cool.
*****
A white couple strolls
with their Jack Russell Terrier.
Early 30s, they glance at the reunion,

asphalt stretching between them. Seem
unsure, cautious
about the reunion taking place. About the bass
dispersing across 7th.

A silent battle taking place
that they don't even realize.
*****
Later, as a young man arrives late,
Dodgers-style interlocking L.A.
on his t-shirt, he hugs
his aunt tightly.

"Hey Aunt Viv. Saved any
of that good smellin chicken
for me?" "Boy you old enough
to feed you ownself."

She rolls her eyes
and shakes her head.

Laughs.

Loving gaze lingering
on her nephew.

"California Love"
now spitting through the speaker.

Those Who Come Before Us

On Sawtelle
I hear Japanese flowing
between the laughter of young friends.
One wears a UCLA sweatshirt. In
Little Osaka. In
West Los Ángeles.

Taiko drums boom
through the parking lot
of the West Los Ángeles Buddhist Temple.
July. Oban.
Sending a message of thanksgiving
to all who have gone before us.

Of immigrants from Wakayama
who created a Japanese fishing village
on Terminal Island,
gone over 40 years
by the time I was born in '84.
Working class families—fishermen—
speaking in their own lingo. Rapid
rough fishermen's talk, blended with
Japanese and English. Nisei children
attending Japanese language school
after a day of learning English
at their public school. Before
executive order 9066
sent them to internment camps.
Internment camps set up for people
who only wanted to build community.

Since the late 1930s,
Japanese basketball leagues
populate the Southern California landscape
where a few of my friends and peers, where
Klaude Kimura, as we graduated

from one LAUSD grade to the next,
can come together as a Japanese community,
where basketball exists as one of the few places
for Japanese American youth
to hang out with other
young Japanese Americans.
Where, at game's end—
heads high, breaths heavy—
they shake hands with their opponents,
sweat dripping from their faces.
Inhabiting gaman.
Some parents bringing game snacks
of rice balls or noodles.

And on Sawtelle I
pass Hashimoto's and Tabuchi's nurseries,
smell the richness of wet dirt,
see the splash of fuchsias'
tiny trumpet shaped magenta flowers,
reminders of when,
in the 1930s and '40s,
Japanese farmed flowers
and strawberries here.

Now, in the early morning, as Angeleños still sleep,
Klaude Kimura,
UCLA grad,
grabs his surfboard,
jumps in his car,
ready to tear up the Southern California waves.

Human Geography

      I

Family research, *Four Generations
of the Dunlop-Dunlap Family*
informs me John W. Dunlap,
my 4x grandfather,
bought a "negro boy
(Jerry)," seven years old.
The same relative who fought
in the battle of Orinsky.
The Revolutionary War.

I sit in the warm Mafundi Institute Auditorium
watching the Watts Village Theater Company's
production of RIOT/REBELLION.
A play when Watts rose
in '65, pushed to fury by cops
traumatizing their lives. White faces
confining their black bodies
to a life they did not choose.

Jerry:
A seven year old boy.
Jerry:
Bought on January 28, 1806.
Ripped from nature's
parental bonds. The safety
of nurture. Alone.

Jerry:
Seven years old.

      II

A deep, full raspy voice
booms through the theater
at Beyond Baroque. Chills
send shivers through my body.
Goosebumps across my

skin. Kamau Daaood using poetry
to channel his ancestral griot,
his people's collective stories.

Daaood cut his teeth
in the famed Watts Writers Workshop,
born from the ashes of the Rebellion
of '65.

Queen mothers and forefathers…
the shoulders that have carried us here.

I'm in love with Daaood's immense power,
his deep projection giving rise
to its Jazz-like melody, turning
traumatic story-songs of his people
into a love for life.

My DNA forever
          stained with hypocrisy.

My need to filter out all
but this Angeleño's words.

My eyes are closed,

ensuring Daaood,
his people,
are not just a single sentence
in the history of the Dunlop-Dunlap family.

At Ocean Park Beach

At Ocean Park Beach,
the setting sun, deep
orange tinging clouds,
a young Latina child
carries a black trash bag
draped over her shoulder, crushed
aluminum cans clanging,
her back hunched, her
feet telling her to
continue on.

An Hour And A Half 'Till Sunrise

I
The sky is still dark;
an hour and a half 'til sunrise.
But Marta's eyes are open and
her feet touch the carpet.
Wisps of street light illuminate
store front signs in Spanish
along the city's commercial spine: Pacific
Boulevard. Huntington Park still sleeps.

Her bones creak as she
stands. Rubs her sleep encrusted
eyes. Another day on the Westside,
Mar Vista Park,
only a cart of cleaning supplies
accompanying the deafening
silence of the gym.

Marta doesn't ask "why this life,"
two busses, an hour and a half
across L.A. County to work.
Not after two daughters, two
quinceañeras, twice shedding tears
as they left for college.

Marta rustles through pages of
La Opinion, the gurgle of coffee
filling the air. Content for
the deep bond she's kept
with her sister, to laugh
with Manuel, her boss,
crow's feet etched in the
corners of her eyes.

II

When she steps onto the bus
at Pacific and Slauson, she has
time to people watch,
to think,
to reflect.

Mostly tired indio and black
faces, hands rough and worn.

As she stares out the window,
sun's rich yellow-white awakening
beige stucco buildings, Marta remembers that,
without money for vacations,
she told her daughters to experience
the world through L.A.: the deep thump
of Taiko drums during Oban; the African
drum circle in Leimert Park; the vibrant
Chicano murals in Boyle Heights.

Marta smiles,
massages her arthritic thumbs,
unwilling to be bitter
about her Huntington Park.
Unwilling to be bitter
that people on the Westside
look at her city,
if at all,
with dismissive eyes.

Who Call This Home

        I

I started hiking Los Ángeles
because of my grandmother.
135 day hikes.
A school teacher engaging me
in the natural world: "What's
this?" she'd ask, a family
hike through the Santa Monicas.
We lost her on Christmas Eve
when I was 5 ½.

Now, my father and I
traverse these mountains. Disappear
from L.A.'s urban sprawl,
from Malibu's new multimillion dollar construction.
Disappear to retrace
his mother's footfalls.

Traveling to other hikes, we've passed
Mary Rindge's house
at Surfrider,
Rancho Malibu's last owner,
who scraped and clawed
through courts,
hired 40 armed guards on horseback
to keep her portion
of the Santa Monicas,
the California Coast,
for only her friends and family.

Once,
    past Surfrider,
while my father and I stood silent
where Zuma Canyon crests,
the Pacific—sun a golden white—
shimmered in the distance. Shared an unspoken connection

with this unique beauty,
mountains a stone's throw from the ocean,
in the place
   we call home.
Where the Tongva
and Chumash fished from canoes,
for abalone.
For sustenance.

We've also hiked Elephant Hill
in El Sereno. Gazing east
over the vast urbanscape
of the San Gabriel Valley, I thought
about how the changing face of America
has made this valley
the first Asian suburbs.
How, alongside Latinos,
they've formed the social ties
that continue to make it their home.

My grandmother made the San Fernando Valley
home for 28 years. My
clearest memory of her
taken from home movies.

135 day hikes.

In the Santa Monicas I've climbed
800 feet with Kelly Hwang and Feroz Rather,
to Eagle Rock in Topanga State Park, sandstone
pitted with crevices and caves. To the north,
an unimpeded vista stretched out,
for mountain lions,
across coastal sage brush terrain. A hike
my father went on with his mother
decades before, struggling to match
her quick, determined steps.

But in 1965, the largest private marina
was constructed over half
of the remaining Ballona Wetlands,
next to where the peaceful Tongva
village of Sa'angna once stood.
Where they constructed their sleeping quarters
of kiiy with branches from the wetlands'
abundant Arroyo Willow, their frames
covered with Tule grass. In the nearby Baldwin Hills,
where I've explored its short steep climb
in Kenneth Hanh State Park,
they foraged for the acorns
of the Coast Live Oak,
for acorn mush.

Yet, after the completion
of the Santa Fe railroad
in the 1880s,
and America saw a real estate empire
across Tongva land,
one Fourth of July,
Kelly and I
saw a doe with two fauns
nibbling on scrub oak
inside Topanga State Park.

135 day hikes.

II

In my history,
when I was in the second grade,
my parents and I trekked Malibu
Creek State Park. We held on tight
to my grandmother's memory

as our footfalls traced paths
she helped clear,
our destination linking generations,
connecting past and present.

The world enveloped us
in chaparral covered slopes,
peaks reaching 2,800 feet
in the mid-distance,
scrub jays
         darting
                past us.

Near the visitors center,
my parents fell into deep contemplation,
my knowledge of this connection
not fully understood. I simply knew
we reached our destination,
where trees we had planted
in my grandmother's memory,
were sinking their roots
into the Southern California soil.
Soil where,
at the steps of the Baldwin Hills
Scenic Overlook, black
and brown faces—slender,
fit, obese—engage in newer
urban cleared trails, reclaiming
a bit of nature for themselves.

Where I hiked down Ferndell in Griffith Park,
135 day hikes,
soft crunch of soil under
my hiking boots, I over-heard
three young Asian American women
discuss the direction of their futures,

remaining here,
in Southern California.

As Griffith J. Griffith said
about this, his land, that now
bears his name, it was
"a Christmas present.
It must be made a place of rest
and relaxation for the masses…
for the plain people."

Like my grandmother.

Like the black and brown
and Asian and Tongva faces
that have sunk their
footprints
in this soil
for generations.

A Roof Over Their Heads

                I
Jorge has reached Mar Vista Park.
The bells attached to his
icebox on wheels announce
the popsicles and ice cream sandwiches,
enticing on a warm
Los Ángeles summer day.

Older siblings and parents
chase children
whose giggles and squeals
permeate the jungle gym. Footprints
upon footprints imprinted in the sand.
Where Spanish mingles with
English and Mandarin. Sprinkled
with Arabic and Hindi.

Here, Jorge wanders, slight hunch
to his gate, silent. He only pauses
to state prices in broken English.
Smiles. Only talks to the parents
who speak his native tongue.
Who speak
Spanish.

                II
Jorge sells ice cream for a simple
smile on a child's face.
He does it to keep worry
and hunger from his sons' eyes. For his sons
to stay children
a while longer.

As Jorge removes his Stetson
and wipes sweat from his brow
he thinks about tomorrow's soccer match

between Mexico and Guatemala.
It's at noon, when children start to rush
and dollars finally accumulate in his palm.

But when a young boy runs up
with a soccer ball tucked beneath his arm,
Jorge sees his sons.
Sees them kick the ball
past the goalie's
diving frame.

Standing beside his icebox
as his sons' rec league game unfolds.

III

Tomorrow, if Jorge leaves early and departs
when the game ends,
he can watch it with his sons,
and still provide a place
where they can rest their eyes,
drift off
till light presents another morning.

Shared Language

Mi novia's abuela watched figures
on her television speak Spanish
as a jet descending into LAX
nearly shook the house.

Lennox, California.
I was 19.
My Mazda's hood smashed
into my windshield.

Now, the television continued to blare Spanish
as Amy Castellanos, my first novia,
communicated with her abuela in a language
they both shared. A language
I frustratingly struggled for three years
to understand. A language
that marked mi novia's abuela as an outsider
in a country where she
cultivated family.

I now
sat in the kitchen, a steaming
bowl of homemade posole
fogging my glasses. Sitting beside Amy,
a new jet rumbled deafeningly
over the roof, swallowed
any language
spoken between these walls. Spoken
in this neighborhood. Swallowed
any simple Spanish
forming in my head.

The homemade posole eased
my unsettled stomach as I heard
Amy speak with love
about her abuela,

in-between the deafening engines.
About her abuela no longer able
   to move this way   and that,
the ache of the years
   in her bones.

Concern about my car
faded to the background. Faded
into the closeness of love.

Additional Acknowledgements

As much as writing is a solitary act of creating stories and narratives, no writer produces a book on his or her or them own. However, I'd first like to acknowledge the following sources that helped me craft many of these poems:

Terminal Island: Los Community of Los Angeles Harbor (Angel City Press, 2016) by Naomi Hirahara and Geraldine Knatz; "Masculinity, Femininity, and Asian American Basketball in 20th Century California" by Ryan Reft (KCET.org); "Part I: The First Americans of Ballona—Origins and Daily Life," and "Part II: The First Americans of Ballona—Food and Plant Uses" by Cindy Hardin and Jane Beseda (Santa Monica Bay Audubon Society blog); *Venice: A Contested Bohemia in Los Angeles* by Andrew Deener (University of Chicago Press, 2012), California's Office of Historic Preservation website page "Serra Springs" and the Wikipedia page "Serra Springs (California)"; *On Gold Mountain* by Lisa See (Vintage Books, 1995); "Guatemalans Aren't Just Fleeing Gangs" by Saul Elbein from the New Republic July 3, 2014; and "Four Generations of the Dunlop-Dunlap Family" by Fanny Dunlap.

A big thank you goes out to *december* magazine and Editor/Publisher Gianna Jacobson, and former L.A. Poet Laureate and contest judge Luis J. Rodriguez for awarding me the 2018 Jeff Marks Memorial Poetry Prize for my poem "Those Who Come Before Us."

Thank you to Leah Maines, Kevin Maines, Christen Kincaid and everyone at Finishing Line Press for believing in my chapbook and in the universal appeal of such L.A. centered poems.

Also big thanks to Mike Sonksen for all your support and encouragement, not only with my writing, but with life. Not only did you assure me my manuscript was on the right track, but while in grad school at Fresno State, your KCET articles on the Los Ángeles literary community sustained my connection to L.A. as I wrote my stories about the city. This was my first connection to the vibrant literary community I would later become a part of.

Thank you to everyone—Alex Espinoza, Susan Straight, Anthony Macías, Francesca Lia Block, Luis J. Rodriguez, Cynthia Guardado and many, many others—for your positive influence that directly or indirectly helped shaped what I write about. This chapbook would look very different, or not exist at all, without you.

Feroz Rather, thank you for your friendship. All through grad school you pushed me to be a better writer, helped shape my opinions on the important role writing plays in exploring the most vital truths, ideas and stories that speak to our humanity, whether positively or otherwise. I still remember all our good late night talks.

Thank you Cynthia Guardado, F. Douglas Brown and Mike Sonksen for reading my manuscript once I had completed a first draft. Your advice helped fill in some of the blind spots I had, that helped take these poems to the next level.

Plus, to the L.A. literary community, for holding space where I can share my truth, my work, in a warm environment. A special shout out goes to former host Jeffrey Martin and Tía Chucha's Open Mic. There in June of 2014 is where I first read my poems, including one that's in this chapbook. I still remember Jeffrey's warm words praising the power of my poems, disbelieving I was a novice poet.

Last, but not least, to my parents: thank you for everything. You never discouraged me from pursuing the writer's life. You ensured I was exposed to writers by taking me to the Los Angeles Times Festival of Books each spring and provided space, after grad school, where I wrote many of these poems. And thank you Mom for being the first and most loyal reader of my work. I am grateful for the advice.

Brian Dunlap is a native Angeleño who still lives in Los Ángeles. It was in the novels, short stories and essays of Susan Straight and Francesca Lia Block where he first discovered the importance of the literature of place, setting him on the path to write about his own place, L.A. He explores and captures those stories that are hidden in plain sight.

Dunlap has created and run the workshop "Los Angeles: Your City," to encourage people to write their own L.A. stories, at such venues as 826LA and the Hammer Museum. He's also mentored young writers at the literary and arts nonprofit DSTLArts and Fresno State's Young Writers Conference.

He's the winner of the 2018 Jeff Marks Memorial Poetry Prize from *december* magazine judged by former Los Ángeles Poet Laurate Luis J. Rodreguez. He's published poems and book reviews in *Angel City Review, CCM-Entropy, California Quarterly and Dryland*, among others. He received BA and MFA degrees in creative writing from UC Riverside and Fresno State, respectively. He runs the blog site www.losangelesliterature.wordpress.com, a resource to explore L.A.'s vast literary culture.

www.ingramcontent.com/pod-product-compliance
Lightning Source LLC
LaVergne TN
LVHW041600070426
835507LV00011B/1205